Original title:
Tulip Tropes

Copyright © 2025 Creative Arts Management OÜ
All rights reserved.

Author: Amelia Montgomery
ISBN HARDBACK: 978-1-80566-692-9
ISBN PAPERBACK: 978-1-80566-977-7

The Quiet Symphony of Nature

In fields of color, blooms do sway,
They gossip gently, come what may.
A dance of petals, a silent jest,
Each flower thinking it's the best.

The bees take notes, with buzzing glee,
As blooms compete for the best cup of tea.
With stems so straight, and leaves so green,
A garden's got talent, if you know what I mean!

The daisies chuckle, the roses pout,
While daisies play tag, the pups run about.
The wind whispers secrets through leafy bows,
While sunflowers strut like they're wearing bows.

In the quiet of nature, the laughter grows,
As petals tickle each other with prose.
With every rustle, a joke unfolds,
In the garden's theater, where nonsense is gold.

Symphony of the Seasons

Spring sings softly, blooms awake,
Colors dance, a joyful shake.
Summer giggles, sunbeams bright,
Petals swaying, pure delight.

Autumn whispers, leaves descend,
Nature's laughter, it won't end.
Winter chuckles, snowflakes play,
Pretend the flowers went away.

Blooms in the Shade

Underleafy canopies, blossoms grin,
Sun's a prankster, can't let them in.
Hiding laughter, petals tease,
Joyful blooms dance with the breeze.

In the shadows, colors beam,
Nature's humor, like a dream.
Petals blush, a cheeky sight,
Underneath the dappled light.

Nature's Brushstrokes

A palette spills on grassy floors,
Dandelions crack jokes galore.
With every stroke, a quirky face,
Art by nature, full of grace.

Brush with pollen, tickle and tease,
Colors giggle among the trees.
Every hue, a playful cheer,
Nature's laughter ringing near.

Echoes of a Flower

Petals whisper secrets sweet,
In the garden, laughs repeat.
Buds burst forth with silly puns,
Nature's fun, never done.

Echoing joy, the blossoms share,
A melody floats through the air.
Every bloom, a jolly tune,
Painting smiles beneath the moon.

Secrets Beneath the Surface

In gardens where whispers play,
The blooms giggle in their sway.
With roots that tickle underground,
They share secrets that abound.

A beetle winks, the worm gives chase,
As petals dance, a wild embrace.
They plot mischief, no doubt dear,
Making pollen puffs appear!

A Canvas of Color

Oh look, a palette spilled and bright,
With splashes of glee in morning light.
Bumblebees can't help but grin,
In this artist's world, we all spin.

Paint me yellow, red, and blue,
Giggles echo, oh what's this hue?
The daisies blush, the roses pout,
Laughing blooms, they dance about!

The Language of Fragile Beauty

Whisper soft, my petals say,
Let's have fun, come out and play!
A daisy's wink, a tulip's nod,
In colors bright, they play the odd.

Flirting blooms with every breeze,
Taking turns to tease with ease.
A flower's laugh is pure delight,
Their fragile charm shines through the night.

Echoes of a Floral Dream

In dreams of petals, laughter reigns,
With echoes bouncing through the lanes.
The violets giggle in the dark,
As crickets join the merry lark.

A rose's joke, a daffodil's grin,
In a field of chuckles, all fit in.
So sprout some joy, let laughter bloom,
In gardens bright, let fun consume!

The Palette of Dawn

In gardens where the colors blend,
A painter's brush, a gentle friend.
With petals bright and leaves so spry,
They dance like ribbons in the sky.

A yellow joke, a red surprise,
As bugs in suits wear tiny ties.
With each new bloom, a giggle starts,
In morning light, they steal our hearts.

Petal Stories

Once a bloom met a sly bee,
"What's your favorite drink?" said he.
"Honey, of course, what could be sweeter?"
"I prefer nectar, it's a great heater!"

They shared tall tales of the sun,
Of how to grow tall and have fun.
In the chatter, a breeze would tease,
Laughter echoed through the leaves with ease.

Ephemeral Beauties

A fleeting glance, a wink of fate,
In nature's show, we celebrate.
Their time is short, they know it well,
Like a comedian with a swell.

With vivid hues and cheeky grins,
Playing tag with summer winds.
They giggle softly, bloom and sway,
A joyful jest made every day.

Blooms of Curiosity

What's this? A petal asking why?
Why does the sun wear a golden tie?
"It's for the parties in the sky!"
A flower chuckles, oh my, oh my!

They ponder deeply, where birds might roam,
And wonder if clouds ever feel at home.
In blooming laughter, secrets flow,
As petals ponder all they know.

Sunlit Reverie

In a garden so bright, the flowers play,
Their jokes take flight with the light of day.
A bee cracks a pun, buzzing with glee,
While daisies all giggle, 'Oh, look at me!'

Sunshine spills laughter, a golden stream,
With petals that dance, they plot and scheme.
A lily declares, 'I'm the star of the show!'
While pansies just smirk, 'We know, we know!'

In the Shade of Blossoms

Under blooms that sway, the humor blooms,
With whispers of wit in the leafy rooms.
A rose makes a fuss, 'I'm the queen, you see!'
But tulips chime in, 'Oh, please, not we!'

The shadows hold secrets, so sly and spry,
As violets chuckle, 'Let's let that one fly.'
A dandelion snorts, burst into a fit,
Nature's own jesters, oh, isn't it a hit?

The Poetry of Petal and Stem

Rhymes in the breeze where the petals do spin,
Each leaf has a story, and a grin to win.
In the garden of jests, the rhododendron sings,
While peonies boast of their colorful rings.

Bumbles and giggles, they frolic and swirl,
In vibrant confusion, the flowers unfurl.
A sunflower winks, with a speech so grand,
While lilacs just chuckle, 'We don't understand!'

Vibrant Visions of Renewal

Life in full bloom, what a comical sight,
As blooms trade their tales in the warm sunlight.
Daisies declare, 'We've got the best view!'
But roses retort, 'Oh, we shine, it's true!'

New sprouts are spry, with mischief and fun,
Sowing the seeds of laughter, one by one.
As nature conspires, with jokes galore,
Each blossom a jest, who could ask for more?

A Portrait of Spring's Embrace

In a field of colors bright,
Flowers dance in sheer delight.
Bumblebees in foolish flight,
Pollinate with all their might.

Sunshine tickles every petal,
While the tulips play a riddle.
Waving to each other's medal,
Garden jokes are truly settled.

Bob the bloom lost in the breeze,
Tried to sway, but missed his knees.
Chasing shadows with such ease,
In a game of flowery tease.

Nature's laughter fills the air,
With blooms that play without a care.
Springtime's wild and quirky flair,
Paints a portrait that we share.

Whispers of the Garden's Heart.

In the garden, secrets hum,
Petals giggle, bees are dumb.
"Did you hear that?" Roses strum,
A tune of chaos, here they come.

Tulips boasting, "We're the best!"
Daffodils say, "We passed the test!"
Sunflowers face the sun, not stressed,
While daisies play at nature's jest.

Vines entangle secrets tight,
A spider's web, a funny sight.
The garden hosts a wild light,
Where each bud chases pure delight.

Whispers float on every breeze,
Nature's laughter, never flees.
In this riot, flowers tease,
Joy blooms wild with such great ease.

Blossoms in Bloom

Blossoms in a riotous trance,
Wiggling leaves join in the dance.
A crooked stem leads the prance,
Nature's world in pure romance.

Petals in a jolly fight,
Color battles, oh, what a sight!
"Red is better!" "No, it's white!"
Amongst them, the laughter's light.

Garden gnomes join the spree,
Sprouting grins for all to see.
With watering cans, they decree,
"Bloom's the best, just let it be!"

Every bud a silly quirk,
As the sun begins its work.
In their bloom, there's much to smirk,
Life's a joke, a happy perk.

Whispered Petals

Whispered petals gather near,
Telling tales we hold so dear.
With twinkling eyes, they co-appear,
Sharing secrets loud and clear.

"Watch me twirl!" a blossom prattles,
In petals, giggles, and those rattles.
Butterflies join in on battles,
In this garden of silly rattles.

Sunshine spills a golden thread,
As flowers bloom above our head.
Comically, they're misled,
Tripping over words they spread.

Little buds with hearts so bold,
In their antics, stories unfold.
Whispered petals, tales retold,
A laughter's rhythm never cold.

The Timeless Embrace of Nature

In gardens bright, the flowers play,
Dancing with the breeze all day.
They wear their hues like fancy coats,
Each one a laugh, as nature votes.

With petals wide, they spin and sway,
A vibrant show, come what may.
They lavish joy on every glance,
Inviting all to join their dance.

The bees are buzzing, oh what fun,
They dip and dive, a lively run.
While critters munch on leafy treats,
Nature's buffet, a grand feast meets.

So come, dear friend, let's join the cheer,
Embrace the blooms that bring us near.
In every petal, laughter streams,
Nature wraps us in her dreams.

An Ode to Flora's Palette

In the garden, colors shout,
A rainbow blooms, there's no doubt.
Each flower's grin, a quirky sight,
Nature's palette feels just right.

Pastel shades and bold, bright hues,
Some pompous, others look confused.
They chat with bees, they wink and tease,
Nature's jesters, aiming to please.

Petunias giggle, daisies fall,
While roses blush, they stand up tall.
A playful brush, a canvas free,
In this floral symphony.

As sunshine drips from leafy trees,
The paintbrush sways upon the breeze.
Here blooms a stunning visual feast,
Whispering joy; the laughter's least.

The Enchanted Garden's Tale

In shadowed nooks, the flowers whine,
"I'm too short; look at that vine!"
They gossip sweetly, side by side,
Plotting mischief with utmost pride.

The sun shines down, they soak up rays,
In petal tiptoes, they do ballet.
A squirrel trips on bright marigolds,
"Oh dear," he sighs, "Nature's so bold!"

They sprout tall tales, sharing delight,
Each bloom a story to excite.
The giggling daisies, with their charms,
Dodge bees and breezes, waving arms.

With every twist and turn we wander,
The colors leave us full of wonder.
A garden mixed with whimsy, fun,
In each petal, laughter's spun.

A Whirl of Colorful Sentiments

In fields where petals float along,
Each color sings a silly song.
Pinks and yellows join the choir,
While purple harmonies never tire.

The daisies play hide and seek,
While tuberoses take a peek.
They chuckle softly, "Who's the best?"
A challenge blooms in garden zest.

Bright sunflowers nodding in the crowd,
Whispering secrets, feeling proud.
While lilies pose with a suave grace,
Nature's beauties, take their place.

So let's skip through this fragrant spree,
Grab a stem, join in with glee!
For in this garden, joy abounds,
In every laugh, the heart resounds.

Garden of Color

In the garden, colors clash,
A pink one trips, oh what a dash!
Yellow laughs at the clumsy show,
While blue grins wide, stealing the glow.

Red and green join in a race,
Who will bloom with the brightest face?
Petals sipping dew like tea,
Gossiping whispers, oh so free!

Butterflies dance, a silly sight,
Frantically swirling left and right.
Bees buzz in with a noisy cheer,
Creating chaos without a fear.

The Language of Flowers

Roses whisper tales so sweet,
Violets giggle during their feat.
Daisies shout, "We're cute, not shy!"
While lilacs float, oh my, oh my!

Carnations grumble, feeling low,
'Why do tulips steal the show?'
Sunflowers mock, 'Just look at us!'
With towering heights, they make a fuss!

Lilies boast of their long-lasting grace,
But tulips just roll, 'It's all a race.'
With petals flapping in the breeze,
Who knew gardens could tease with ease?

Secrets Beneath the Soil

Underneath the dirt, they chat,
Worms and roots in a huddle sat.
'Why does the onion cry so loud?'
The carrots chuckle, feeling proud.

Secrets shared with twinkling eyes,
'Who spilt the juice?' a beetroot cries.
Seeds giggle in their cozy beds,
Dreaming of sprouts and leafy heads!

The gossip flows through tangled vines,
'What's the scoop on the daisies' lines?'
While moles dig holes to eavesdrop clear,
In this world, the laughs are near!

Dance of the Petals

Petals swirling on a breeze,
Twisting, twirling with such ease.
Petal party? Yes indeed!
A whimsical, colorful stampede!

Sunshine joins to light the scene,
While shadows giggle; what a dream!
Ladybugs tap to the beat,
As daisies stomp their tiny feet!

What's that up with tulips high?
Are they peeking at the sky?
With every sway and every spin,
Who's the winner? Let's begin!

Blooms of Desire

In the garden of wants, petals twirl,
Each bloom a secret, a playful whirl.
The colors chatter, in whispers they say,
"Pick me, oh pick me, let's dance today!"

Beneath the sunlight, they strut and tease,
Waving their heads in a breezy breeze.
A clash of hues in a silly parade,
Planting a smile where worries had laid.

With mischief in colors, they play their part,
Do they bloom for love or just for art?
In this quirky patch, nature's comic relief,
Each flower a punchline, each laugh a belief.

So when you wander through petals and leaves,
Remember the humor that nature weaves.
For every pretty bloom that makes you swoon,
There's laughter afoot, beneath the warm moon.

Colors of a Dream

In a dream, colors wiggle and play,
Dancing around in a whimsical way.
Pinks and yellows, oh what a sight,
Chasing each other, from morning to night.

Scarlet giggles and violet sighs,
Sprinkled laughter that reaches the skies.
"Come join our party!" the daisies call,
While the shy little green shoots sit quite small.

Every petal, a joke wrapped in cheer,
Turning up faces, inviting good beer.
A splash of orange, a wink from the blue,
As they tease the wind, "Are we funny to you?"

In this dream garden, mirth does abound,
While colors conspire all over the ground.
So pick up a hue, let your worries seam,
And dance with the laughter that flows in your dream.

Essence of Eden

In a land of joy, where flowers conspire,
They giggle and bloom, a colorful choir.
Blossoms with sass, in a frolicsome way,
Whispering hints of a bright, funny day.

Each blossom like gossip, in breezes they float,
Trading their tales on a bright petal boat.
"Who wore it best?" asks the stylish rose,
While the shy lily blushes, "I suppose!"

Beneath the blue skies, laughter runs free,
With petals like clowns, what bliss it must be.
The daisies are jesters, the tulips all weave,
Such humor in growth, in the joys we believe.

In Eden's essence, the joy's overflowing,
With silly little blooms in the wind, they are blowing.
So join in the fun, let your spirit glide,
For the essence of laughter is found here inside.

Resplendent Moments

In the garden of giggles, moments resound,
Each bloom a delight, laughter is found.
Bright colors unite, in a comical tale,
As petals all chatter, with nary a fail.

"Look at me wobble!" shouts sunny marigold,
While purple pansies snicker, a sight to behold.
Jokes sprout like weeds, the tulips all beam,
It's a resplendent moment, like living a dream.

With petals like pages, they tell silly lore,
Each one an actor, forever wanting more.
"Why did the bee land?" they buzz with a grin,
"To taste all the nectar and sweet up the din!"

So revel in moments that burst with delight,
With flowers as jesters that brighten the night.
For in every garden, there's joy to uncover,
Resplendent in laughter, like no other lover.

Spring's Silent Symphony

In gardens bright, they softly sway,
Like dancers lost in youthful play.
With petals wide, they catch the breeze,
While sneaky bees sip with unease.

Their colors clash, a riotous climb,
A painter's joke in springtime's rhyme.
They whisper secrets to the sun,
"Do we look silly? Oh, this is fun!"

A bloom so bold, a sight to see,
Waving at you, just look at me!
With cheerful grins, they say hello,
And laugh at grass that's far too low.

Beneath the sky, they strike a pose,
Admiring each other, no one knows.
In nature's play, they steal the show,
These charming jesters, row by row.

Painted Faces of Nature

In colors bright, they wear their crown,
Like happy clowns in a bustling town.
A splash of pink, a dash of gold,
A sight to see, their stories told.

They wink at bees that buzz around,
"Can you believe the joy we've found?"
With petals wide, they charm the ground,
In laughter's bloom, all lost and found.

A sunny prank, they come alive,
With every breeze, they dance and strive.
"Look at us! We're quite the sight!"
They giggle softly, hearts so light.

And in this patch of fun and glee,
They poke at roots and tease the trees.
"Oh watch your step," they tease and play,
As springtime blooms in wild display.

The Elegance Beneath the Sun

With graceful bows, they hold their heads,
As sunlight glimmers in their beds.
Dressed in gowns of red and gold,
They strut about, so proud and bold.

"Look at us shine, we're quite the scene!"
They giggle at clouds, still rather keen.
In floral frolics, they sway and spin,
Feeling like champions, ready to win.

A dainty dance, a floral parade,
In nature's circus, they are unafraid.
"Catch our drift?" they playfully sigh,
As wind whispers softly by.

Together they laugh, a joyous crew,
Matching in style, in every hue.
For beneath that sun, life's all in jest,
In gardens where elegance meets the best.

A Tapestry of Blooms

In a patchwork quilt of hues so bright,
They gather round for a flower fight.
"Bet you can't catch me!" one shouts with glee,
As petals scatter, wild and free.

They tease the grass, they tickle the air,
In nature's laughter, all find their flair.
A canvas woven with cheer and grace,
Every bloom wears a smiling face.

With playful twists, they chase the bee,
"Onward! Catch us, if you can, we plea!"
In this riot of colors, they laugh and prance,
A haven of joy, a whimsical dance.

Together they thrive, in sunlight's glow,
Painting the world, stealing the show.
In a tapestry of blooms, they unite,
A joyful ruckus, a pure delight.

Shades of Transience

In the garden, blooms parade,
Laughter dances, colors invade.
Petals nod, a quirky show,
Whispers of the winds that blow.

Hues of pink, and yellows bright,
Jokes exchanged in morning light.
Nature's jesters, bold and spry,
Tickling bees that wander by.

Fleeting moments, here they thrive,
Poking fun, they seem alive.
With each breeze, a giggling call,
A short-lived prank, they rise and fall.

At twilight's blush, a soft farewell,
Balloons of petals, tales they tell.
Waving hands, their time is short,
In vibrant laughs, they take their port.

In the Company of Flowers

Here they gather, flowers bright,
Mimicking the stars at night.
Chatter fills the sunny bloom,
As bees bring honey, sweet perfume.

Petal hats on all their heads,
Making jokes on garden beds.
In the breeze, they toss and tease,
Fashion struts, they aim to please.

Season's jesters, bold and merry,
With bumblebees, they play like very.
Ticklish stems and soft-edged vines,
Laughing 'neath the weathered pines.

When rain arrives, they duck and dive,
Splashes of humor, they arrive.
Dripping joy, a playful spree,
With rhymes of nature, wild and free.

Nature's Gentle Echo

Mirthful echoes in the vale,
Petals giggle, tell their tale.
With each rustle, laughter grows,
In tiny crowns, their secret glows.

Sunshine tickles through the leaves,
Making mischief as it weaves.
Witty lines on leafy pages,
Nature's script, through all the stages.

In the shade, a jest unfolds,
Silly antics, springtime molds.
Colors clash in comic spree,
Witty roots in harmony.

As shadows stretch, they find their fun,
Chasing light, they seldom run.
Echoes dance in foamy hues,
Nature's laughter, bright and true.

The Brush of Spring

In springtime's art, with colors bold,
Silly strokes, laughter unfold.
Brush of bright, they flaunt and sway,
In this gallery of play.

Whimsical splashes, pinks and golds,
Canvas of stories yet untold.
With every petal's playful glide,
Spring's gallery opens wide.

Breezy giggles, dainty and spry,
With a wink, they let out a sigh.
Dancing hues on a laughing wind,
In joyous chatter, their art is pinned.

As they brush, they tease and tease,
Nature's light, a warm, sweet breeze.
Laughter echoes through the green,
In spring's embrace, they're all unseen!

Secrets of the Garden Path

In the garden, secrets hide,
Whispers of petals wait inside.
Bumbles buzzing, hops so spry,
Tickled toes and snoozing flies.

A gnome with a grin, oh what a sight,
Interrupting tea for a silly fight.
Socks mismatched in mud-soaked glee,
Dancing tulips, wild and free.

Old sun hats tossed amidst the bloom,
Chasing shadows while bees consume.
Laughter echoes through the green,
A joke-telling frog, the garden's queen!

With every step, a giggle found,
In this whimsical world, joy abounds.
Petal pranks and stories spin,
Secrets held in laughter's din.

Radiance in Stillness

Blooms beam brightly like cheeky kids,
Cracking jokes, and flipping lids.
Stillness holds a giggle close,
Sunshine winks, and petals dose.

Butterflies wear tiny clowns' shoes,
Sharing humor in vibrant hues.
A gentle breeze, it whispers low,
"Why did the flower stop? It's slow!"

Spouting puns with pollen charms,
Roots that rumble and arms that disarm.
Amid the stillness, laughter swells,
In this radiant pocket, joy dwells.

Mirror-like ponds reflect the jest,
Nature's laughter, truly the best.
Serenity draped in silken threads,
Cracking smiles, no need for beds.

Blossoms and Reflections

In a mirror pond, blossoms play,
Reflecting giggles throughout the day.
Petals poke fun at frogs that croak,
With full bellies, they share a joke.

The sunbeam pranks the sleeping leaves,
Tales of mischief, no one believes.
Swaying stems in rhythm clink,
Floral friendships that rarely stink.

A bumblebee with a bowtie bright,
Dancing petals, what a sight!
They gossip 'bout weeds and embarrassing spots,
Leaping with laughter, connecting the dots.

In nature's mirror, reflections gleam,
Blossoms laughing like a sweet dream.
With every ripple, joy is found,
In this garden where smiles abound.

Melodies of the Meadow

In meadows wide, the jokes take flight,
Singing flowers bask in light.
A cricket's chirp, a punchline bold,
Nature's stage, a story told.

Daisies wear crowns of silly spins,
While grasshoppers join in the violin.
"Why did the flower bring a guest?"
A riddle told, a giggle's quest.

Poppies painted with laughter's brush,
Twirling in a joyous hush.
The daisies make silly faces wide,
Underneath the sunny tide.

With each breeze, a giggle swirls,
Melodies dance, like merry pearls.
In this meadow, joy's the theme,
Laughter's echoes, a beautiful dream.

The Mirror of Nature

In a meadow where daisies dance,
A dandelion takes a chance.
It's spruced up in a wispy gown,
Wishing to twirl, not just sit down.

Bumblebees wearing tiny hats,
Complain about the gossiping cats.
The sun giggles, throws a ray,
As flowers argue who's the most 'bloom' today.

A butterfly holds a fancy soiree,
Inviting all critters to feel sway.
They sip nectar from crystal cups,
While ants do the conga, shaking their ups.

The breeze whispers secrets in the trees,
As spiders weave tales with glittered ease.
Nature's mirror shows us delight,
With every petal leading to laughs all night.

Palette of Nostalgia

A splash of color spills from the past,
As memories bloom, they sure hold fast.
Crayons and laughter blend in the air,
Making every moment seem quite rare.

Garden gnomes reminisce in their spot,
About wild parties they nearly forgot.
Daisies recall their summer spree,
Clinking their glasses of honeyed tea.

The tulips giggle, a funny crew,
Wearing boots of polka dots—who knew?
They dance in rhythm, a colorful sway,
While dreams of rainbow slides come out to play.

A palette thrown on the canvas wide,
Sprays of joy we can't seem to hide.
With laughter echoes and shadows where,
Nostalgia blooms, it's a comedy fair!

In the Garden's Embrace

In the garden where the oddballs roam,
Each peculiar plant claims its home.
A carrot in shades of electric green,
Complains of discrimination, it's quite the scene.

Roses blush as they spot the sun,
While peonies hold court, having fun.
The hydrangeas gossip under the dew,
Trading tales of who sprouted anew.

Worms wear spectacles, thinking they're sly,
Plotting adventures, oh my, oh my!
The daisies giggle, soft and bright,
As the moon takes over, preparing for night.

In this embrace, all quirks feel right,
A carnival of petals, joyous and light.
Each corner filled with cheerful grace,
In the heart of the garden, there's always a space.

Petal Reveries

In a whimsical dream, petals take flight,
Chasing the moon through the velvety night.
A daffodil dreams of playing the flute,
While the tulip trains as a dancer in boots.

Sunflowers twirl, their heads held high,
As daisies trace circles, reaching the sky.
Pansies tell jokes that ring oh so bright,
These petal reveries spark pure delight.

A lily flips pancakes with utmost grace,
While violets serve tea at their own little place.
Butterflies waltz in a shimmering haze,
In these dreamy gardens, forever they'll blaze.

A serenade hums through the whispering leaves,
As petals join hands, what joy it weaves!
In the land of reveries, laughter prevails,
In every sweet bloom, a story that sails.

Blooming Emotions

Petals giggle, swirling round,
In colors bright, joy can be found.
Whispers of spring tickle the air,
Nature's dance brings laughter to share.

Roots in the ground play hide and seek,
While bees buzz jokes in a sunny week.
Dandelions laugh, with crowns held high,
As butterflies flutter, oh my, oh my!

Sunshine beams, a silly grin,
While shadows play, they join in spin.
The breeze blows softly, teasing the blooms,
Painting the garden with giggly tunes.

With each new bud, a story's spun,
In a field of laughter, life is fun.
Each bloom a giggle, wild and free,
Nature's own jesters, filled with glee.

Kaleidoscope of Flora

Look at those flowers, what a sight,
Dancing in colors, oh what delight!
Yellow and pink, they tease the bee,
"Catch us if you can!" they laugh with glee.

Leafy comedies on the vine,
"Tell me a joke, it's your time to shine!"
Petals in patterns, a quirky show,
A garden parade, come see the flow!

Worms wear hats, as they munch their feast,
"Why was the plant so well-dressed?" they teased.
"Because it had roots and a flair for style!"
The laughter of nature will last a while.

In this patch of joy, all's jolly and bright,
Every bloom plays its part with delight.
A riot of colors, each one a gem,
This floral circus is a whimsical realm.

The Poetry of Gardens

In gardens where giggles never cease,
Daisies write verses with such finesse.
Laughter woven in every leaf,
Bringing joy to the world, a sweet relief.

Roses recite with a posh little flair,
While sunflowers grin, waving in the air.
"Knock, knock!" they call, with humor so grand,
All of nature lends a helping hand.

Crickets compose songs of silly delight,
As huddled leaves gossip deep in the night.
The moon looks down, chuckling with stars,
A tapestry rich, with heavenly bars.

Thus the garden offers, rich in jest,
A symphony of green, a blooming fest.
With every seed sown, a tale anew,
The poetry blooms, in laughter's hue.

Colors in the Wind

Colors flutter, tickling the breeze,
Nature's laughter, rustling through trees.
"Catch me if you can!" the lilacs shout,
As vibrant hues swirl about.

Can you see the butterflies, all dressed up?
Their fancy outfits fill nature's cup.
Winking flowers, with whimsical charm,
In this land of color, none come to harm.

The wind plays tricks, a playful tease,
Spinning blossoms, tossing with ease.
"Do you believe in magic?" they chime,
"We bloom with joy, we dance with time!"

So come and play in this vivid earth,
With every petal, discover rebirth.
Colors in the wind, a ballet grand,
Nature's pure laughter, at our command.

Impressions of Spring

In a garden, petals dance,
Wearing colors that entrance.
Bumblebees buzz, with style so bold,
Making pollen exchanges, stories untold.

The sun plays peek-a-boo with the sky,
While frisky breezes swoosh by.
A ladybug, with a royal flair,
Claims the best seat, without a care.

Daffodils gossip, tulips giggle,
As lilies try their best to wiggle.
Nature's humor, light and free,
Spring's whimsical comedy, joyfully we see.

With every bloom, a playful jest,
Where flowers bloom, smiles manifest.
So let's frolic in this vibrant hue,
And keep laughing 'til the blossoms are through.

Inflorescence

In a cluster, they gather 'round,
Chit-chatting, near the ground.
Petal pals, in shades so bright,
Organizing a jest-filled night.

A bud slips and lands with a *thud*,
While another claims, "Oh, what a dud!"
The daisies snicker, the violets cheer,
As each new bloom brings springtime near.

With pollen-coated pranks galore,
They vow to play just a bit more.
A garden party, with laughter loud,
Nature's circus, so fun and proud.

In the breeze, a laugh takes wing,
The petals jiggle—oh what a thing!
Amidst the colors, joy expands,
As friendships bloom in leafy bands.

Whispers of Time

Once upon a blossom's breath,
Time tickled petals until their death.
Each layer, a wink, each leaf, a giggle,
Nature's clock runs wild with a wiggle.

Buds arguing over their morning dew,
"Mine's shiner!" "No, mine's more true!"
A drama unfolds, with roots entwined,
In this leafy saga, humor's defined.

While the sun blinks down, it can't avoid,
The tiny antics that the blooms enjoyed.
The world pauses, to hear their chatter,
As bees debug the latest flower matter.

Oh, to bloom at time's own pace,
Each moment a chance to embrace
The silly whims of living greens,
In nature's watch, laughter gleans.

Flora's Interlude

Take a bow, oh flowers proud,
Your colors shout, your scents are loud.
In the spotlight, they flaunt and twist,
A floral comedy that can't be missed.

Sunflowers strut, with tall, bright grins,
While ferns curl up like they're in a spin.
A sneaky squirrel joins the show,
And steals a bloom, putting on a glow.

In this garden, every petal's a star,
With breezy giggles echoing far.
The daisies dance, the poppies prance,
Creating a ruckus in nature's romance.

So here's to blooms, with quirks galore,
In Flora's world, laughter's the core.
Let's cherish each chuckle, sprout, and giggle,
In this whimsical bloom, let our hearts wiggle.

Echoes of the Orchard

In the orchard where laughter flies,
Fruit hangs low while the birdies cry.
A pear tried to dance, but slipped on its peel,
The apples just chuckled, 'Oh, what a deal!'

Sunflowers gossip, their heads held high,
They trade silly secrets that tickle the sky.
A squirrel cartwheeled, trying to impress,
But rolled off a branch in a fluffy red dress.

A beetle in shades thinks he's quite the dude,
But trips on his own shine, oh what a mood!
While peaches throw parties with jam and delight,
The pears just stand back, trying to act bright.

Laughter and giggles amongst dark tree trunks,
With critters that stumble and jitter like punks.
In the orchard of joy, where all things align,
Every twist of a vine comes tangled in wine.

The Heart of the Meadow

In the meadow where daisies play peek-a-boo,
A bumblebee buzzed, 'I think I like you!'
But tripped on a petal, flew up in a whirl,
Crashing down softly on a giggling girl.

The rabbits are dancing, not shy to reveal,
Their tap-dancing moves, oh what a big deal!
But one little bunny forgot the last beat,
And tumbled headfirst into the tall wheat.

A butterfly painted in colors so bright,
Tried to impress but fell out of sight.
With a laugh from a ladybug perched up real high,
She said, 'Let it shimmer, don't flutter and cry!'

As pollen flirts with the breeze in the dance,
The ants are debating, 'Did you see that chance?'
To roll in the sunshine and stretch out their legs,
While the grasshoppers joke about one-legged pegs.

Kaleidoscope of Life

In a garden so wild, colorful blooms collide,
A flower tried singing, but lost all its pride.
With a stanza so silly, it tickled the bees,
Who laughed till they wobbled and fell to their knees.

A sunflower sashayed in a flowery gown,
But rustled her petals and frolicked around.
While tulips wore hats pretending to be hip,
The daisies just giggled and gave them a quip.

The violets debated about who's the best,
As the bees took a break; they needed some rest.
'You're royal!' said one, 'With colors so fine!'
'But you've got the fragrance!' 'Oh no, it's divine!'

And as the sun dipped, casting shadows and cheer,
The crickets began their nightly debut here.
In this kaleidoscope, where life laughs and spins,
Every petal a story, where silliness wins.

Whispers of the Bloom

In a field where whispers float like the breeze,
The roses are blushing, the daisies tease.
A cheery old daffodil told a tall tale,
About how the thorns once ran a flower sale.

The lilacs are laughing, they twirl in delight,
While petals are arguing who'll bloom through the night.
One stubborn bud said, 'I'll bloom when I please!'
And a bumblebee buzzed, 'You'll see, if you sneeze!'

With butterflies boasting of wings like a car,
Stumbled on a stem and crashed—oh how bizarre!
A ladybug winked, 'You're dazzling in flight!'
As she added, 'But landing? Oh, what a sight!'

As laughter drifts gently on each lovely wave,
The blooms all conspired to rise from the grave.
In this garden of giggles, where joy comes to loom,
It's a party of colors, painted bright in full bloom.

When Petals Dance with Light

The petals sway in silly glee,
They twirl and jig, oh can't you see?
With colors bright, like a clown's silly hat,
They laugh with the breeze, how about that?

A bee buzzes by, thinks he's a star,
Tripping on nectar, he's gone too far.
He bumps into a bloom, with a wobbly spin,
"Watch out!" they giggle, "It's nectar's twin!"

Dancing daisies join in the fun,
Frolicking flowers under the sun.
They sway left and right, a floral parade,
A vibrant spectacle, nothing's delayed!

And as the day ends, they snicker with pride,
For tomorrow they'll dance, wide-eyed and spry.
When petals meet light, oh what a sight,
In the garden of laughter, everything's right!

The Elegance of Velvet Blooms

A bloom in velvet, soft and smooth,
Acting all posh, oh what a groove!
"I'm elegant!" it boasts with flair,
While snickers erupt from the flowers nearby, aware.

The daffodils yell, "What a pretentious show!"
As the velvet petal puts on its glow.
But deep down inside, they all do agree,
That plush little bloom is a sight to see!

A gust comes to play with a cheeky intent,
The velvet one flops, looking quite spent.
With a tumble and roll, oh what a mess,
It giggles and sighs in its floral dress.

Yet amidst all the fancy, there's laughter that blooms,
For elegance shines in the quirkiest rooms.
In the garden of jest, where flowers all thrive,
Each petal holds beauty, keeping smiles alive!

Nature's Brushstrokes

With a palette so vibrant, nature paints wide,
Strokes of humor on the flowers they hide.
Here a splash of yellow, there a dab of pink,
A daffodil giggles, gives the tulips a wink.

The lilacs are laughing, tickled by the bees,
As they flit and flutter, buzzing with ease.
A dandelion puffs, sending seeds on their way,
"Catch me if you can!" it dares them to play.

The roses, all smug, in their thorns do delight,
"We're the best dancers, just watch us tonight!"
But a clumsy old bee, on their petals collides,
And the laughter erupts as he flounders and slides.

So nature's brushstrokes create joy all around,
With colors and chuckles in the garden abound.
For each little bloom, in its unique mix,
Brings laughter to life with its delicate tricks!

Blooming in Soft Hues

In a patch of giggles where soft hues reside,
The flowers all whisper, with humor as their guide.
They bloom in shy shades, pink, lavender too,
"We're the quiet ones, but oh how we do!"

A shy little bud pops out of the ground,
"I'm bashful but sassy! Come see what I've found!"
With petals like pouts and a soft, sweet allure,
It joins in the fun that all blooms must secure.

A daisy chimes in, with a glint in its eye,
"In this colorful chaos, let's give it a try!"
They sway and they twirl, with delicate grace,
A floral ballet, in their whimsical space.

So blooming in soft hues brings joy to the day,
Where laughter and colors create a bouquet.
Every flower a creature, each petal a muse,
In this garden of giggles, let's all share the views!

Memories Carved in Petals

In gardens where the blooms do sway,
A petal slipped and danced away.
It chased a bee, oh what a scene,
A floral dance, both bold and keen.

The petals giggle, bright and loud,
While ants march by, a bustling crowd.
One flower yawns, the wind does tease,
Waving to bees with such great ease.

A curious bloom made quite the fuss,
As bumblebees hopped on a bus.
In their hats, they seemed so grand,
Traveling flowers, a merry band!

So take a tip from nature's crew,
To find the joy in skies so blue.
Memories made on a sunny day,
In petal whispers, we laugh and play.

The Seasonal Serenade

Spring sings softly, flowers burst,
But winter's chill is still rehearsed.
A frosty bloom with shivers slight,
It chuckles loud, 'Just wait for light!'

Summer's here, the petals beam,
'Time to party, life's a dream!'
With sun hats on, the daisies dance,
While tulips wobble, taking a chance.

Autumn calls, a funny sight,
Leaves tumble down, a joyful flight.
A squash invites the flowers near,
With pumpkin jokes that make them cheer!

The seasons change, they twirl and sway,
With flowers laughing all the way.
In nature's jest, we find delight,
Each bloom, a giggle, pure and bright.

Beauty in Transience

One blossom flaunts, with gusto grand,
But soon it wilts, it's close at hand.
A fleeting blush upon the stem,
It winks and sighs, 'Don't forget them!'

The petals know just how to tease,
'Look at us, we sway with ease!'
But soon they flutter, drift away,
Like secrets shared at the end of day.

Laughter echoes through each hue,
As blossoms dream of morning dew.
They whisper tales of love and fun,
In fleeting moments, joy begun.

So cherish blooms that quickly pass,
Their funny ways, a cheeky sass.
For beauty thrives in shades of change,
Each petal's laugh, a sweet exchange.

Laughter of Flowers

In a field where colors blend,
The flowers giggle, no need to pretend.
With buzzing bees exchanging jokes,
They share their wit, both wise and hoax.

A daffodil cracks a clever line,
While asters laugh at the sun's design.
They poke at clouds, with silly grins,
In a garden theater, where fun begins.

The tulips poke their heads up high,
'There goes the sun, oh my, oh my!'
With fluttering petals, they catch the breeze,
While daisies delight, bringing everyone ease.

So join the laughter; let it flow,
With every bloom, a joyful show.
In nature's riot, we find our way,
Where flowers frolic, and don't delay!

The Harmony of Blooms

In a garden, colors clash,
Petals argue, oh, what a splash!
One shouts red, the other blue,
Dancing petals, what a view!

Bees buzz in a frantic race,
While snails move at a slower pace.
Bunny hops with a silly grin,
In this garden, chaos wins!

Sunlight spills on leafy greens,
Plants gossip, sharing scenes.
A flower lifts its leafy head,
"Who's the brightest?" it said.

With laughter, blooms intertwine,
Every hue a funny line.
In this wacky world of cheer,
Garden's charm, oh dear, oh dear!

Verses Amidst the Vines

Vines twist like a dancer's spin,
Hanging grapes, let the feast begin!
One grape bursts, juice flies wide,
Laughter echoes, can't hide!

A gopher peeks, with eyes so round,
Hoping for a snack he found.
But tripping on a vine so fine,
He joins the dance, oh how divine!

The sun throws shades, it's quite a game,
The flowers can't find whom to blame.
With every bend and every twist,
A movable feast, can't be missed!

So let us sing with glee and cheer,
In the garden, nothing's clear.
With roots that jiggle and leaves that jive,
In this viney world, we thrive!

In the Garden's Light

In the morning, sunbeams play,
Daisy's wink, it's a cheeky day.
Butterflies wear outfits bright,
Fashion shows in pure delight!

Bees in suits, so neatly pressed,
Buzzing helps them feel the best.
A ladybug dons polka dots,
"Who wore it better?" Oh, the plots!

The wind plays tunes, a breezy jest,
Leaves twirl around, it's a silly fest.
Grasshoppers join in, cracking jokes,
While worms groove to the music, folks!

As colors blend in joyous mix,
Nature laughs, throwing tricks.
In the garden, where humor blooms,
Life's a party, dispelling glooms!

Embrace of Springtime

Spring arrives with a bounce and jig,
Frogs wear crowns, feeling big.
They croak in chorus, quite the show,
A royal ball, don't you know?

Colors pop like popcorn fun,
Flowers giggle, the race has begun.
A butterfly flits, in floral gowns,
A mingle here, then flops down!

A carrot slips, lands with a fluff,
Saying, "Hey, I'm good enough!"
Gardeners chuckle, rake in hand,
Nature's humor, oh, so grand!

In spring's embrace, we share a grin,
With every bloom, the laughter spins.
So let's rejoice, let spirits soar,
In this garden, we adore!

Palette of Serenity

In the garden where laughter grows,
Colors dance as the soft wind blows.
Petals giggle in a bright display,
Whispering secrets of the day.

Bees in tuxedos buzz around,
Painting pollen without a sound.
Laughter blooms with every hue,
Nature's jest, a grand debut.

One petal's dressed in polka dots,
While others prance in comical spots.
The sun's a jester, bright and bold,
Casting shadows, stories told.

So join the fun, let colors play,
In the fields where smiles sway.
With nature's brush, we find our glee,
In this vibrant tapestry.

Pastel Promises

In pastel realms where giggles sprout,
Bunnies hop and squirrels pout.
Colors clash with playful cheer,
As daisies wink, drawing near.

With every shade, we make a pact,
To find the joy in each abstract.
A peachy blush and minty grin,
Making mischief, let's begin!

The tulip twirls in a silly dance,
While daisies join in without a chance.
Leaves rustle like laughter flowing,
In this world where fun keeps growing.

Whimsical dreams in soft pastels,
Underneath the lavender bells.
Come play a while in hues so bright,
Where laughter sparkles in the light.

A Dance of Colors

Colors whirling in a raucous spree,
Jumps of joy, just wait and see.
Crimson flirt and buttercup tease,
In this garden, hearts find their ease.

A flamboyant fuchsia takes the lead,
While shy lilac sprouts the seed.
Each petal's laugh a silly sound,
In the midst of joy, we're all spellbound.

Marigolds sway in the summer's glow,
With poppies marching to and fro.
They twirl and spin in the warm sunlight,
Creating a canvas, pure delight.

So join this vibrant, playful show,
Where colors dance and laughter flows.
In this merry, painted thrum,
No worries here, just joy to come!

Nature's Soft Serenade

In fields where whispers tickle the air,
Nature sings tunes without a care.
Golden hues and green so bright,
Crafting a symphony of pure delight.

Petals sway in rhythmic time,
Chortling secrets, oh so sublime.
In the chorus of bright blooms swell,
Nature whispers its funny spell.

The daisies play hide and seek with breeze,
While sunflowers wave with comedic ease.
Every color shimmies with grace,
Creating smiles in this joyful place.

So let us frolic in nature's song,
Where each color dances all day long.
In this soft serenade, we find our cheer,
Laughing together, spreading the cheer.

Threads of Floral Narrative

In gardens bright where flowers sway,
The blooms engage in cheeky play.
They whisper jokes in colors bold,
A riot of tales yet to be told.

Petals giggle, roots do dance,
Each stem's a player in this romance.
With sunlit smiles and dew on leaves,
They craft the tales one hardly believes.

With bumblebees as jesters near,
The blossoms buzz with laughter clear.
A tulip in a tutu spins,
Proclaims that floral fun begins!

So join the blooms, let's play a while,
In fields awash with cheerful style.
For in this patch of green delight,
Floral narratives take flight.

A Tapestry of Colorful Lives

In patches bright where colors clash,
The flowers mingle, making a splash.
A daffodil with a cheeky grin,
Says, "Life's too short to wear the same skin!"

The daisies gossip with painted grace,
While violets sip tea, holding their place.
Roses roll eyes at the tulip's flair,
"You're too flamboyant, do take care!"

A sea of laughter in every hue,
With petals dancing, laughs anew.
Each bloom a story, short and sweet,
Creating memories in sun's warm seat.

So gather close, let's laugh and cheer,
In this playful garden, bring your dear.
For life is a tapestry, woven bright,
With every bloom a story in sight.

Blooms that Stole the Heart

There once were blooms that loved to tease,
With playful jests, they aimed to please.
A sunflower winked, its seeds a grin,
While tulips plotted where to begin.

The daisies dared the bees to dance,
While tempted by a bright romance.
Each fragrance wafted, swirling around,
In this floral circus, joy was found.

A poppy quipped about the bees,
"Those buzzing fools, bring me to knees!"
While lavenders shared their calming tales,
In spite of yawns, delight prevails.

So let these blooms break all the charts,
With laughter stitched in gentle arts.
For every petal, grin, and sigh,
These flowers steal your heart, oh my!

Where Springtime Stories Blossom

In springtime's grasp where stories flow,
The blossoms gather for a show.
With petals fluffed and colors bright,
They host a party, what a sight!

The crocuses crack jokes in the sun,
"I'm the first here, let's have some fun!"
Tulips boast of their vibrant flair,
While poppies dream without a care.

The dandelions scatters seeds with glee,
"Come spread our tales, wild and free!"
While pansies mix their shades and hues,
Crafting tales you won't refuse.

So gather round, let laughter swell,
In this bloom-filled world, all is well.
For where these blooms and stories play,
Springtime's laughter lights the day.

www.ingramcontent.com/pod-product-compliance
Lightning Source LLC
Chambersburg PA
CBHW071827160426
43209CB00003B/219